ISBN 0-87666-925-9

CONTENTS

PHOTO CREDITS

Photography by Mervin F. Roberts, Dr. Herbert R. Axel-
rod, Louise Van der Meid and by the staff at T.F.H. Mr.
Ray Hanson supplied most of the color photographs
and information for the captions. The front end pages
show a pair of guinea pigs with miscellaneous immature
specimens to show the diversity of color available in
modern cavies (guinea pigs). The back end papers show
mature specimens of the Dutch variety. The title page
shows a pet cavy being fed its daily vitamins.

Distributed in the UNITED STATES by T.F.H. Publications, Inc., 211 West
Sylvania Avenue, Neptune City, NJ 07753; in CANADA by H & L Pet Supplies
Inc., 27 Kingston Crescent, Kitchener, Ontario N2B 2T6; Rolf C. Hagen Ltd.,
3225 Sartelon Street, Montreal 382 Quebec; in ENGLAND by T.F.H. (Great
Britain) Ltd., 11 Ormside Way, Holmethorpe Industrial Estate, Redhill, Sur-
rey RH1 2PX; in AUSTRALIA AND THE SOUTH PACIFIC by T.F.H. (Australia)
Pty. Ltd., Box 149, Brookvale 2100 N.S.W., Australia; in NEW ZEALAND by
Ross Haines & Son, Ltd., 18 Monmouth Street, Grey Lynn, Auckland 2 New
Zealand; in SINGAPORE AND MALAYSIA by MPH Distributors Pte., 71-77
Stamford Road, Singapore 0617; in the PHILIPPINES by Bio-Research, 5
Lippay Street, San Lorenzo Village, Makati, Rizal; in SOUTH AFRICA by
Multipet Pty. Ltd., 30 Turners Avenue, Durban 4001. Published by T.F.H.
Publications Inc., Ltd., the British Crown Colony of Hong Kong. THIS IS
THE 1983 EDITION.

Guinea Pigs

by Kay Ragland

The guinea pig, or cavy, is an ideal pet for adults and children alike. Guinea pigs are quiet, clean, easy to feed and breed, docile, small and inexpensive.

The Guinea Pig As A Pet

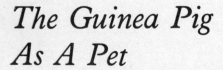

Among small animals that make excellent pets, the guinea pig certainly rates an important place, especially for youngsters or invalids, and for several reasons. First, the guinea pig is a beautiful animal with lovable manners and cute ways; second, he is easy to care for and feed; and, third, even when handled too roughly, he will not bite. So, given the few necessities he may need in the way of food, housing, and plenty of affection, he will make you a most desirable pet.

This creature is neither a pig nor does it come from Guinea! Actually, it is a rodent from South America, first domesticated by the Incas of Peru who used it mainly for food purposes. Evidently, some of the little animals were taken by English and Dutch slave traders to Guinea and then on to Europe, which may account for the name of *guinea pig*. The only connection with a pig is a low grunt made when the animal is hungry. They also produce a sort of whistle which, if you can duplicate it, makes a most interesting conversation (even though you may not know what your pal is trying to tell you). More accurately, he is called a *cavy*, but it is doubtful if you went into the majority of petshops and asked for a cavy, anyone would know what you really wanted.

The cavy comes in a variety of sizes and colors, ranging from a tiny specimen the size of a rat, to a huge sized animal, the size of a small dog. There is one type that lives on barren desert plains and one that lives in water. Their ability to adapt themselves makes their range from low to high, dry to moist climates.

Aside from being a wonderful pet, this animal has gained himself honorable service in scientific laboratories, especially in the isolation and propagation of bacteria and the production of serum. Its ability to breed rapidly makes it ideal for the study of heredity and thus it is found in schools and colleges as well as laboratories. Selective breeding has produced several strains and modifications from the original.

(1) The guinea pig may well be the most popular of all laboratory animals. It has even given its name to any animal (including humans) used for experimental purposes. (2) This cavy weighs just over 6 ounces, including some of its food. (3) This Peruvian lady raises and sells cavies for food. Cavies are domesticated in Peru and are bred for size. The Peruvians find them to be ideal food animals, since they eat almost anything vegetable in origin.

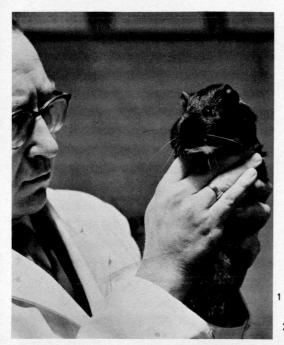

1

2

3

Pet cavies come in a variety of colors. (1) The color has nothing to do with its pet qualities, but the more "fancy" the cavy the more expensive to buy. Many children are started out with a "pair" of young cavies (2) which are colored alike. But there is no reason why two different varieties of cavies (3) shouldn't be the beginning of a collection for a youngster. As they mature, though, the cavy-lover (4) might want something in a more exotically colored cavy like a Tortie and White.

2
3

4

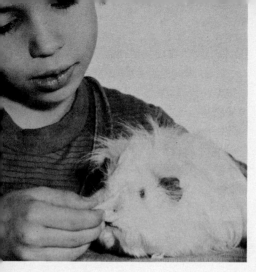

There are three popular varieties of cavy as far as coat or fur is concerned. The English short-hair is a shiny, fine-textured coat (shown below right). The cavy in the middle is an Abyssinian rough-hair. Its coat is made up of rosettes that give it an unkempt appearance. The cavy to the left, below, is a Peruvian long-hair. The longer the hair, the better. Excellent specimens even have their faces completely covered.

Varieties

Coat type and color determines the variety of guinea pig. Although there are many varieties, three are best known and found in pet stores. These are the *English short-haired,* The *Peruvian long-haired,* and the *Abyssinian rough-haired.*

The English variety is probably the best known and the most common, having short hair which is very glossy and fine in texture. It ranges in color from mixed black, white, brown, chocolate, and reds to solid colors, with a wide nose, open ears, long body, rounded rear, and brilliant and curious eyes. Extremely hardy, this animal needs little attention for the care of his coat.

(Above) The underside view of a Tortie and White cavy. (Right) A long-haired Peruvian cavy chewing on a daisy! Cavies eat most vegetable matter.

The *Peruvian* resembles an animated mop and is usually considered show stock. The soft hair can attain a length of several inches and cover the entire body, often even over the eyes. As the guinea pig has no tail, it is hard to determine on this variety which end is which. Some Peruvians have long, silky hair over the body but short hair over the face. This variety needs practically daily combing to keep the beautiful coat free of mats, and to keep the animal looking its best. My first experience with this Peruvian type was a visit to a guinea pig breeder. We were having lunch on an enclosed patio when suddenly what I had thought was a fuzzy rug rolled up, started to move—bundles of long silky hair propelled themselves across the room toward us—no visible movement of legs, no eyes, in fact, just a furry bit of animation, coming to the table in search of whatever was proferred. When he picked up one, it immediately ran up his arm to his shoulder where it perched. When no food was forthcoming, it gave out little squeals, which got louder as they were ignored.

Beautiful as this variety is, don't get one unless you are prepared to properly care for it, which means brushing and combing, otherwise you will have an unkempt pet—he cannot care for himself.

The last of the better known guinea pigs is the *Abyssinian*, a truly beautiful animal with a rough, wiry coat resembling somewhat any of the wire-haired breeds of dog, but with one outstanding exception. The hair of the Abyssinian is made up of swirls, like cowlicks, which are called *rosettes*. The more rosettes, the better. In competition, the rosettes are actually counted. Eight seems to be an ideal number. Combing and brushing intensifies the coat condition. Owners of this variety will insist that it is much more intelligent than other guinea pigs. Be that as it may, I have found them all intelligent.

The Sheltie is a new breed of guinea pig; it was recognized as a standardized breed in 1973. It is a mutation of the Peruvian cavy and looks like one except that the hair grows differently. It has a smooth face, but the hair from the head grows down like a mane which looks like a full, silky textured coat. It does not have the rosettes of the Abyssinian or the Peruvian, and its head is blunt rather than pointed. It comes in all colors and is a beautiful looking animal. This cavy is a favorite, but as the hair is so long and silky, it needs constant care and grooming and the dedication of a saint to brush it every day.

As for coloration, guinea pigs are available in solid colors of black, white, brown, red, chocolate, reddish brown, and in mixed combinations. The various color combinations are:

A young Sheltie, or Silkie as it is sometimes called, has a more blunt face and a beautiful long coat that requires daily grooming unless you keep it trimmed (use a dog clipper for the purpose).

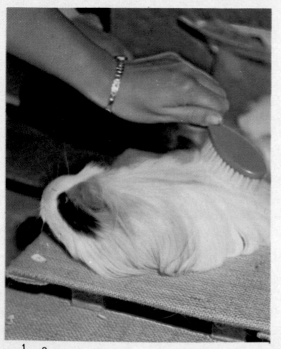

(1) The Sheltie (Silkie in the U.S.A.) requires daily grooming with a soft brush. (2) A black Himalayan cavy. They are colored like Siamese cats, but they are born white and change colors within six months. (3) More and more rare colors are showing up. Chocolate Dutch with red eyes is still very rare. (4) Tortoiseshell and White cavy. (5) A Peruvian cavy. It differs from the Sheltie in the hair styling. The Peruvian has hair that is combed over its face, while the Sheltie has its hair combed from head to foot, leaving the face visible.

1   2

3
4

5

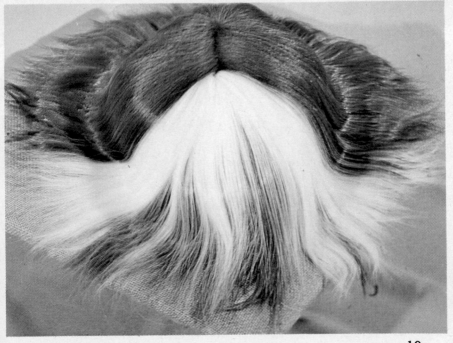

19

Himalayan—white body with nose, ears and feet of black.

Tortoise Shell—patches of dark and light brown, practically alike in size, and distributed all over the body. The different colors should be very definite and not running or blending into another color.

Tortoise and White—three colors, the tortoise shell coloration with definite equal areas of white. Colors should be clear and concise, and not run into one another.

Dutch—white with a pattern of dark or reddish brown or tan.

Brindle—intermixed dark and light tan coloration.

Agouti—there are two kinds, the **Silver** has a shimmering silver-coloration with grayish underside; the **Golden** has the dark hairs tipped with yellow.

Self-color—as the name indicates, there is but one solid color, be it black, white, brown, cream, red, white or tan, with black eyes.

Albino—pure white with pink eyes.

Standard Classifications and Color in Cavies

The Abyssinian

The Abyssinian Cavy, or "Abby" as it is usually called is probably the most popular of the Non-Self varieties. It is an ideal breed for beginners as it does not require the show preparation necessary for other breeds like the Peruvian, the Agouti, or the Self. The Abby is a very active creature that bristles and bustles about, never happy to be still. Breeders talk a language of their own for a breed that is unique in its makeup; such things as furnishings, mane, collar ruff, saddle, ridges, hip rosettes, and rump rosettes.

The placing of the ridge is very important, if they are correct then the rosettes which come between the ridges will be straight and well-placed, and in this breed only the harsher the coat the better.

At the small shows the various colors are usually entered in one class but at the larger shows and particularly the Abyssinian Stock Shows the colors are split up into classes.

BRINDLE is an intermixing of red and black hairs

TORTOISESHELL is a patching of red and black

ROAN is an intermixing of Black/Grey and White

STRAWBERRY ROAN is a mixing of Red and White

TORTOISESHELL AND WHITE is Red, Black and White markings

SELF COLORS include Black, Red, and White, and some of the rarer markings are the Agouti and Himalayan.

The distribution and mixing of patches, roaning, or brindling has nothing to do with the requirements of the smooth coated breeds of the same name. In the Abby the patching or mixing of color is not considered, it must merely carry the color or colors of its respective type. However, an allowance of 5 points is made in the standard because some of the colors can be poor, a black should be black not a rusty black and red should not be a faded red. Although it is said that no good Abby can be a poor color, if two good ones were tying for first place at a show and one had a stronger color this would be the decisive factor.

Of all the colors, the Brindle usually has the harshest coat and selfs the softest. Harshness must be bred for, it does not come from keeping them in colder atmospheres as is popularly supposed.

The main part of the body is called the saddle. There should be four rosettes across and round the middle of the body, running around the back in an arc, one on each side and one on either side of the backbone ridge. Further back over the hips are another four rosettes, one on each rump

(1) The Golden Agouti female suckling one of her young. She also had an albino baby because her father was an albino and the mother of her mate was an albino. Her litter was composed of an albino, a Golden Agouti and a pied or mixed color youngster. (2) and (3) The Tortoise and White is probably the most beautiful of all cavies with its stark red, white and black. This is almost a perfect specimen. The two views of the same animal (2) and (3) show that the patches are basically square with straight lines between each color. The homologous patches sidewise are matched; that is, the black patch on the left side is represented by a white patch on the right side, while the red patch on the flank is balanced by a black patch on the other side. See the color photograph on page 14 for an underside view of this same cavy.

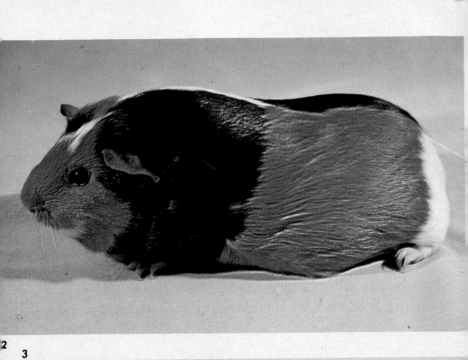

2

3

23

and one on each hip forming an arc over the back quarters. All the rosettes should be deep and start from a pin point center. Poor ridges will make rosettes look flat and will be penalized. Rosettes on the rump are inclined to run in what is called guttering or channelling, and sometimes a rosette will be a split or double rosette. The ridges divide the rosettes and should be stiff and upright, not flat. The ruff or collar ridge goes around the shoulders behind the ears. The main ridge runs between the ears and down the center of the back. Flatness of this, particularly the section from the ears to the ruff, or mane, is quite common in otherwise good exhibits due to shortness of coat. Flatness of this ridge behind the ruff is often due to shortness of coat and lack of shoulder substance. The upstanding ruff, mane, and moustaches or furnishings are immediately noticeable when you first look at a good specimen and they give the crisp bristling appearance.

When purchasing a trio of Abbys, the boar should be the one of highest quality and as near the standard as possible. A double rosette is not such a bad fault as flatness of ridges, rosettes, or missing rosettes. The sows should also be good but slight faults are acceptable, indeed all cavies have some fault, perfection being that which we all strive to achieve.

Because of his sex the boar will have the harsher coat and is usually the show pig. For this reason it is very wise to keep a number of good boars, do not make the mistake of relying on just one and do not attempt to breed and show the same boar. If you show your boar frequently he may go sterile, as showing can upset him. If you keep a number of boars you can show occasionally and breed frequently from each one.

When babies are born they will show their rosettes, ridges, and furnishings, but these are inclined to go quite flat after a day or so and indeed almost disappear, returning again around weaning time.

It is particularly important to keep your stock free of lice because they can cause the rosette centers to become open and scurfy and the hair to fall out. Heating foods such as maize should not be fed as this could also cause the same trouble.

The standard for all colors is: (American point scores in left column, English in right)

Rosettes	25	20
Ridges	---	20
Coat (this refers to harshness)	20	20
Shape and size	15	10
Head furnishings and Mane	10	15
Color	15	5
Eyes and Ears	5	5
Condition	10	5
Total:	100	100

Agoutis

Golden and Silver are the two main colors, but Chocolate, Cinnamon, Lemon, and Salmon are occasionally seen. Agoutis are generally big, bold, and very fit animals with a bright, glossy appearance. The Golden should be a rich mahogany color interspersed with black ticking and having a narrow golden strip up its belly. The chest, legs and feet are ticked as the body. The coloration of the Agouti is only at the hair ends and does not go down to the skin.

The Silver has a narrow silver/grey strip up the belly whilst the rest of the body, head, chest, legs and feet are silver/grey evenly ticked with black.

Evenness of ticking is of prime importance and this should extend to the feet, on which many fail by being too dark. Shading and patchiness can occur and is to be penalized.

Silver Agoutis differ from the Goldens when breeding as

1

(1) Wild guinea pigs from Peru, where they are called cuis (kwees). They live on grasses, like miniature cows. (2) This Golden Agouti has a very deep blue-black base color, though its hairs are ticked with gold. This type of fur makes expensive fur coats! (3) You can allow your cavies the freedom of the garden, but don't be angry if they chew up your favorite flowers! (4) This Peruvian cavy is being "color fed" carrots. Some breeders think that the reds are intensified if carrots are fed to the cavy. No definite conclusion has been reached on this point.

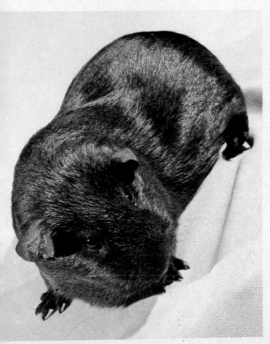

2

3

4

27

they sometimes have what are called "dilutes" in the litter. These are non-ticked cavies that look somewhat like a self black. Dilutes are useful in the breeding pen to darken color when silver to silver matings are producing stock that is too light. Dilute to dilute is not recommended.

Different shades of Silver and Golden are produced and some are useful in producing the desired show color. When purchasing your initial stock your supplier will give you some pointers on this subject. Ask him to show you how to groom out the long guard hairs, a show requirement.

When breeding the following are prime faults to watch for:

Eye circles. This is where the ticking does not go right up to the rim of the eye, only the main body color which makes the eye appear to have a light circle of color around it.

Excessive white hairs in the body, white toenails, uneven ticking, dark feet, side whiskers, light chests and chins are faults. Special attention must be given to color.

The standard for all colors is: (American point scores in left column, English in right)

Color	15	20
Evenness of ticking throughout	30	30
Shape	20	20
Eyes large and bold	10	5
Ears well shaped and drooping slightly	5	5
Size combined with quality	5	5
Coat	5	5
Condition	10	10
Total:	100	100

The Tortoiseshell and White

Usually referred to as the Tort and White. This is a breed for the sportsman and it is surprising how often breeders of

Dutch are also breeders of Tort and Whites. They are sportsmen because the gamble of producing one near the standard is to some extent a matter of luck, though years of dedication to line and clean patches free from brindling must play a major part in producing these highly attractive, but often exasperating animals. It is a bright, dazzling animal displaying its three colors of red, black and white brilliantly contrasting in squares or patches up one side and down the other in a different color sequence.

It is seldom that one is bred really near the very exacting standard, but the clarity and clear cut lines of some of the squares has to be seen to be appreciated. Others have their colors in patches rather than in squares, but they too are most attractive.

It is important that the colors are good, the red must be deep not ginger or brassy looking, the white dazzling, and the black jet.

The aim is to get the three colors alternatively patched up one side with a dividing line up the middle of the back and to repeat the patched effect down the other side but in a different sequence, the same going under the belly to a line up the middle. There are a number of combinations of the three main colors and the patches can be more than three, but too many patches do not give quite such a distinctive appearance as the three clear and distinct colors.

The standard calls for a head that is half one color and half one of the other colors, running in sequence with the other patches. This is extremely difficult to obtain and many Tort and Whites have the familiar wedge of the Dutch marking with the rest of the face black or red.

The main faults to watch for are brindling and belts of color or bands of color. There are many ways to breed for Torts and Whites, but in all cases clear patching is the main goal to aim for and these animals are selected for breeding. You can breed only from the best you have and try to improve and use those that have patching or plenty of color

(1) A Crested Sheltie. The rosette on the top of the head makes it a "crested" as it is identical in all other ways to a normal Sheltie. (2) Two selfs, a black and a lilac, peeking out of a box in which the were shipped. (3) A Tortie and White Abyssinian. (4) young white Peruvian lor hair.

4

31

about them well distributed. It is so seldom that one is bred that can conform to the standard, but anything that comes anywhere near the standard is able to be shown. Although as previously mentioned dedication to lines and patches must be the main object when breeding, it has been found that the two most unlikely mismarked mates can produce quite a good specimen, probably because there has been a continuity in their own breeding and while not correct themselves they have passed on their inherent qualities.

The standard for all colors is: (American point scores in left column, English in right)

Patches to be clean cut, clear and distinct	20	25
Equal distribution and uniform placing of patches	30	25
Color	10	20
Shape and size (broad shoulders, Roman nose, shapely ears)	15	15
Eyes	5	5
Coat	10	5
Condition	10	5
Total:	100	100

Faults: Cavies being short of any colored patches on either side shall be penalized.

Side whiskers: A tuft of hair standing out just behind the jowl.

Band: A patch of color going round the body.

Belt: A patch of color going part way round the body.

The Himalayan

This is an interesting breed because its extremities are dark and its body color white. The babies are born white and the pigment on the legs begins to show through in a few days although the points are not totally dark until about 5 to 6 months old. The two colors seen in this breed are Black and Chocolate. The Black is not as dark as the Self Black, but the nearer to this the better. The Chocolates are a milk chocolate shade. The body on both should ideally be white, but this is very hard to achieve together with really dark points. The darker the points the harder to get a really white coat. Many are creamy rather than white and some are very muddy in color and inclined to be patchy.

Breeders usually refer to this breed as "Hims." The dark nose is called the "Smut" and should be quite large and extend up the nose between the eyes, and lower down should spread into the whiskers. The smut is worth the most points individually so the larger and denser this is, the better. The ears should be a matching color, of good shape and drooping, not standing up in the air. The feet or "the points" as they are called must be dense and the color go well up the leg but not beyond the hock.

The show life of the Him is rather restricted as young ones under five months do not have the dense points which are not usually fully through, being interspersed with white hairs which disappear as the animal approaches 5 to 6 months of age. Adults start to lose density and the white hairs again begin to appear as they age. The density can also change from day to day and it is said that a knock or injury can cause the color to temporarily go white.

The standard for the **Black** Himalayan is: (American point scores in left column, English in right)

Nose even and jet black	15	25
Feet—jet black	10	20
Ears—shapely and jet black	10	10
Density of markings	15	---
Coat—short and silky and pure white	10	20
Size and shape	15	10

Eyes—large, bold, ruby red	5	5
Condition	10	10
Color—pure and even in colored sections (Coat and color in English)	10	---
Total:	100	100

The standard for the **Chocolate** is: (American point scores in left column, English in right)

Nose even and rich milk chocolate	15	25
Feet—rich milk chocolate	10	20
Ears—shapely, rich milk chocolate	10	10
Density of markings	15	---
Coat—short, silky and pure white	10	20
Size and shape	15	10
Eyes—large and bold, ruby red	5	5
Condition	10	10
Color—pure and even in colored sections (Coat and color in English)	10	---
Total:	100	100

The Peruvian

This is the long haired member of the Cavy family. An adult in full show coat is a superb sight and a credit not only to careful breeding but also to the patience and perseverance of the owner who must be prepared to brush and rearrange the long hair every day. More care and attention must be lavished on the Peruvian than any other breed. It is a full time occupation to breed and show Peruvians. It is not a beginner's cavy, but is one that fascinates a great many fanciers, many of whom unfortunately seem to take them to intermediate stage and then give up. This is understandable because the standard requires the hair to be soft and silky yet very dense, and the softer and silkier the coat the harder it is to keep free from tangles.

Not all Peruvians have the temperament to sit still on their special show boards when being judged, or waiting to be judged at a show. They have to do this so as not to spoil their long coats which can grow up to 20 inches (50 cm) or more. It is reckoned the coat grows 1 inch (20 mm) in a month and the longer the coat grows the more likely it is to break and become thin at the ends. The animal itself can undo in seconds the work of months, by tangling it hair, losing a wrapper which keeps the hair bound up, or by chewing a piece of hair, so a great deal of thought must go into the decision to breed Peruvians for showing.

Peruvians that are used for breeding must have their long coats cut off and cut very short around the back end and around the genitals, in order that they can mate. The coat should be cut short regularly so that the animal can move about with ease and not become entangled in its own fur. During the summer the coats are cut as short as possible so that the animal does not suffer from heat exhaustion. Show animals with their long coats and wrappers should be kept in a well ventilated position in the caviary to be kept as cool as possible in the extremely hot weather. In the winter, of course, the coat serves as a very good means of keeping the cavy warm and can be allowed to grow down to its feet on breeding stock.

When Peruvians are born they are short coated and should have two rosettes sited on the rump, but the hair does not grow towards the rump but towards the ears, the opposite direction to the other breeds, only the hair below the rosettes grows downwards. As the animal matures the hair will start to part up the middle and should be encouraged downwards on each side of the parting. Eventually the hair is brushed over the two rosettes into what is called the sweep. When long enough, at about three months old, it is taken up into what is called a wrapper made of paper and a small piece of balsa wood and secured with a rubber band. At about 5½-6 months of age the side hair is put into side wrappers, one on each side. This is where problems can start as these are inclined to come out rather easily, though when the hair becomes longer they do stay in better. If the wrappers are not put in with great care they can cause the animal to chew itself. Provided the wrappers are comfortable and the animal is given sufficient hay which must be cut into lengths of about 3 inches (75 mm) and pressed well down to stop the cavy from burrowing underneath it, chewing should not occur. Boredom is probably the cause of this because show Peruvians must be kept on their own. Lice can also cause irritation which will make a Peruvian scratch its fur out.

The hair over the Peruvian's face is called the frontal fringe and this is probably the hardest to breed for. Many lack on frontal, and it is also the most difficult part to keep long and dense and the most likely part to become chewed. It can be seen therefore that the Peruvian fancier has a challenge before him that depends not quite so much on breeding but on his own tenacity.

The standard for all Peruvians, which come in a variety of colors, is: (American point scores in left column, English in right)

	American	English
General appearance— broad shoulders, firm flesh, clear eyes	10	5
Fringe, with hair completely covering the face	13	15
Shoulders and sides	13	15
Texture to be of a silky nature	13	20
Density of coat	13	15
Sweep, length and fullness, the hair falling over the hindquarters	13	15

Condition	15	5
Color (in English,		
Head 5 pts., size 5 pts.)	10	10
Total:	100	100

The hair should be fine, silky and glossy.

The fringe should be furnished so that the hair hangs in a thick mane on each side of the head.

The face should be short and the eyes large and full.

While we aim for a straight coat, a slight wave should not be unduly penalized.

If the sweep is slightly longer than the sides, this does not constitute uneven length.

Young Peruvians are very large for their age, much bigger than even some of the Self breeds. Their age is usually determined when being shown by the length of their coat and therefore taking into account that it usually grows at 1 inch (25 mm) a month the top hair will give an indication of the age.

The Sheltie

This is a new breed of guinea pig that was recognized in Great Britain in 1973 but has only now been recognized in the U.S.A. under a different name. The "Silky," as it is known here, was shown in Houston, Texas in 1977 and as the presentation was excellent and of such a high standard, the Board of Directors waived the time it would normally have taken to standardize the breed.

The Sheltie or Silky is a long haired breed rather like the Peruvian, but the hair grows differently. It has a smooth face and the hair from the head grows down like a mane which is carried along the body to join a sweep like the Peruvian. The Sheltie does not have the hip rosettes like the Peruvian. The head of the Sheltie should be blunt, not pointed, They are an easier breed to manage than the Peruvian as they require only one wrapper to keep the sweep in order. They have no middle parting, the hair is swept back over the body just falling around the shoulders like a cloak. They do not have fringe hiding their faces and this is part of their appeal, their pretty faces can be seen when they are set up on their special show board. As with the Peruvian they must have the temperament to sit still and be shown and are trained to do this as babies.

Type, texture, and density are very important and the colors are varied and very attractive.

The standard for the Sheltie (English) or Silky (American) is: (American point scores in left column, English in right)

	American	English
Head: Broad with short nose and large prominent eyes with hair lying towards the rump	10	10
Mane: Sweeping back to join with sweep and is not parted	13	15
Shoulders: Broad with hair slightly longer continuing along the sides of equal length	13	20
Coat: Silky texture and good wealth of coat at sides	13	20
Sweep: Length and fullness of hair falling over hindquarters (sweep generally to be longer than sides which should be even in length)	13	20
Size:	10	5
Condition and Presentation	10	10
Density:	13	---
Color:	5	---
Total:	100	100

All colors and mixings of colors are acceptable. White is the hardest to keep as staining around the rear end can spoil for showing.

The Crested Cavy

This is a new breed accepted by the National Cavy Club but formerly under the guidance of the Rare Variety Cavy Club. This is a variation on the Self Cavy but cannot be called a Self because it is not smooth, it has a rosette which is placed between the eyes and ears. It is called the English Crested Cavy because in England it is allowed to have the crest or rosette the same color as the body while in America it is only accepted if it has a white crest on a colored body or a contrasting crest to the body color.

The crest is to radiate from a center point between the eyes and ears. The crest is to be a deep rosette, the lower edge is to be well down the nose. Any different colored hairs in the crest are to be severely penalized as in self cavies.

The American Crested must have a crest contrasting to the body color. The crest color to be as near to a complete circle of solid color as possible. A circle of less than 75% is to be severely penalized. The crest color should not appear elsewhere on the body. A blaze of the crest color is to be severly penalized. Hair of body color in the crest is to be penalized. Although this American Crested is extremely attractive, it is also extremely difficult to breed with just the color contrast in the crest.

Himalayan Crested and Agouti Crested Cavies are also making their appearance.

The standard for the English Crested Cavy is: (American point scores in left column, English in right)

	American	English
Crest: to match body color	20	20
Color: to conform to the colors of the matching self	20	24
Shape: short cobby body, deep broad shoulders	20	20
Coat: short and silky	10	12
Ears: rosepetal shaped, set slightly drooping with good width between	5	8
Eyes: large and bold	5	8
Condition:	10	8
The crest rosette	10	---
Total:	100	100

The Self Varieties

A "Self" Cavy is an animal that is the same color all over and is smooth coated. The same standard applies to all the breeds of self cavies and the allocation of points is identical, the only difference being in the requirements of color.

Self Breeds (or varieties)
Short, smooth haired self colored
Self Black
Self White
Self Cream
Self Golden
Self Beige
Self Lilac
Self Red
Self Chocolate

As can be appreciated, color is a very important part of the Self's makeup. Many have good top color but it is not always carried right down to the skin. Texture of coat must be soft and silky, not harsh and coarse. In both cases breeding and careful grooming are the only ways to achieve this.

Type is another very important factor and this includes the shape of the head and the body. The makeup of the head should be bold, broad and blunt, the sow having the better type than the boar. The body should be cobby and square in the shoulders and deep and broad. As we go through the breeds it will be seen that some self breeds excel more on some points than on others.

Eyes must be big and bold, not small and deep set or fatty. This latter condition is a problem to the self breeder seen when the lower lid falls away from the eye and a white/yellow fatty lump develops. The ears should be large and drooping, not standing to attention. Condition is most important in the appearance of the Self cavy and although only 10 points are given for this, the difference between a fit animal and an unfit one is so obvious that no matter how good the type and the color if it is not fit it cannot make up a loss of 10 points.

The standard for the Self Cavy is: (American point scores in left column, English in right)

Color: deep and rich	30	30
Shape: short cobby body, deep broad shoulders, roman nose	25	25
Coat: short and silky	10	15
Ears: rose shaped, set slightly drooping with good width between	10	10
Eyes: large and bold	10	10
Condition:	10	10
Feet: to match body	5	---
Total:	100	100

The standard color requirements will follow each breed as we go through them.

The Self Black

The Self Black Cavy is indeed beautiful, its supremacy is borne out by its continued success and popularity over many years. More than any other breed of Self it can come nearer to the standard for shape and type and color and has taken more Best in Show awards than any other breed of cavy. Because the sow has the better shaped head and a softer coat she is the show pig; boars are a little more pointed in the face, but they must have very broad, bold heads and a really good one can sometimes beat a sow.

As much is expected of the Self Black, there is a great deal to breed for and competition is very strong; producing a real "Flyer" is no easy matter, particularly breeding them consistently which is what you have to aim for. It takes time and it takes patience, but when you see a real good one set up on a box, you will know what is meant.

Faults that must be watched for are crinkly ears or a folded hem on an ear. Some Self Blacks tend to be rather small, but a good one should have good size and substance and be of good shape, not long and narrow on the shoulder. Although the standard does not mention size, the competition is so great that the Self Black must have that something extra in order to win.

You will not go far wrong if you go to a breeder who has established a record of consistency over the years and take the advice that is given to you. Feed them well, treat them kindly and they will give you a lot of pleasure.

The standard requires the color to be black, deep, and lustrous, the same going down to the skin. Eyes to be black.

The Self Cream

This is another breed with exceptionally good type and shape. It has deep ruby eyes which set off the cream color to perfection. There are a number of different shades of cream, in some parts of the country the preference is for a darker and in other parts for a lighter cream. As the name suggests, it should be the color of cream. A dark cream is inclined to be a bit strong or even brassy and too light a cream rather insipid. The main problem is undercolor which is much paler than the top color. Whether this is due to the introduction of Self Whites in the breeding is a question on which breeders seem to differ greatly.

Evenness of color is very necessary and this is difficult to obtain if the undercolor is too light as it will give the coat a patchy, flaky, uneven appearance.

Skill in breeding is required for the litters contain different shades of creams and you cannot just keep breeding light to light; some of the darker ones must be used to keep a good even color throughout the stud and therefore the advice of an experienced breeder must be sought when first starting on this very attractive cavy.

The standard requires: CREAMS should be a pale even color with undercolor to match and free from lemon or yellow tinge. Eyes ruby.

The Self White

This is a very popular breed which like the Self Black has excellent type with the lovely blunt head. The Self White normally seen is the pink eyed Self White but black eyed Whites are now accepted as a standardized breed and are usually exhibited in the same class as the pink eyed.

While the Self White has the beautiful shape of head, it does not have the same shoulder substance as the Self Black. Ears tend to be rather small and crinkly or bend at the edges which spoils the overall appearance. This is a fault which must be carefully watched in the breeding pen as it is a very dominant fault.

It is surprising the different shades of white that can be seen in a line up of whites on the show bench, and although this breed does not have any trouble with undercolor as it is white all the way to the skin, the shades of white can vary from yellowish to greyish but the really snow white exhibit stands out. The coat must be soft and silky, some whites tend to have rather coarse coats although these are not seen as often as they once were and a great improvement has been made in this direction. The large baggy exhibits are rarely seen now, the coarseness has been bred out and the shape improved but some are inclined to be rather long and snaky. The black eyed White is also improving but pigmentation of the ears and pads of the feet has to be watched and eyes that are not truly dark but more ruby must be taken into account.

The Self White must be presented for showing without a mark or stain on its coat and achieving this is far from easy. Constant attention must be paid to the bedding so that the pen never becomes dirty, thus staining the coat particularly on the underside and around the vent. When transporting them to shows the travelling boxes must be carefully wiped to ensure that no dust or dirt can mark the coat, and at the show itself it is wise to wipe thoroughly the wire pen in which the animal will be placed. This is a beautiful breed but an everyday one, not just a weekend one.

The standard requires: WHITES should be pure snow white throughout, ears and feet to match body. Eyes pink (or black).

The Self Beige

This is usually a very big, bold breed of cavy. The standard states the color should be that of real beige cloth, but there are many shades of beige cloth. It is, therefore, a color that will be fixed in the mind and aimed for after seeing a good colored beige cavy. Usually the light medium colored beige with a slightly pinkish overtone is the preferred

44

shade. Undercolor is usually good but evenness of color must be bred for. The eyes of this cavy are pink.

Unfortunately type is not as good as in the black, white, or cream, and it is a much longer shape. Although the boar has not quite such type as the sow it is he who is usually the show animal because he keeps his shape better than the sow who is inclined to become baggy around the belly, particularly after being bred from, although of the two she will, of course, have the better type. Different shades of beige are produced in the litters and skill is needed to select those that will blend together to produce required beige. Dark colored animals should be used in your breeding program, so do not discard those youngsters and keep only the lighter ones or you will find that patchy offsprings will result, some having dark lines or bars on the coat. When born youngsters are quite dark but lighten as they mature. The ears must be carefully smoothed down into a drooping position as they are inclined to have rather "fly away" ears.

They are rather long in coat and as the standard requires a short silky coat, careful attention must be paid to their show preparation for they are not easy to groom and the coat can soon become ragged and broken looking. Light colored cavies tend to suffer from "broken back" which means breaks in the fur and scurfy skin which is usually caused by lice or the feeding of food that is high caloric. Attention to diet is essential; maize and other high calorie foods should be avoided and strict attention given to lice infestations.

The standard requires: BEIGE should resemble real beige cloth with ears and feet to match. Eyes pink.

The Self Golden
The color of this cavy should be that of an old golden guinea, although in fact it varies from brassy yellow to almost pale red. However, once having seen a really good golden cavy the color becomes fixed in your mind and adds

up to a very pleasing animal. They have pink eyes, are usually big bold animals, but seem to have lost the lovely type that they once had. Many today are the correct color which goes right down to the skin but type and coat quality does not seem to have improved which is a great pity. There are still one or two breeders with Goldens of good type and it is worth trying to obtain some of their stock if you intend breeding this popular color. Young Goldens are very dark when born and for this reason are not usually showable until older.

The color of the feet is sometimes somewhat lighter than the body color and this must be considered when breeding as it is a fault penalized on the show bench. Because of the different opinions as to color it is well to aim for type and provided the coat is even in color right down to the skin and not brassy then you will not go far wrong.

The standard requires: GOLDENS should be a rich golden shade with no suggestion of yellow. Ears, feet, and toe nails to match body colour. Eyes pink.

The Self Lilac

This breed is another of the big bold type of self. The color is difficult to explain and has to be seen to be fully appreciated; it can best be described as a dove grey with a pinkish tinge. It is sometimes mistaken for Beige but when the two breeds are side by side, there is no resemblance, the lilac leans towards grey while the beige to fawn. Under color is usually no problem but grooming and preparing the coat is very important and can do a lot to improve their makeup as they are rather long coated and the texture slightly inclined to coarseness. Youngsters are very dark when born, and lighten as they grow. Barring and patchiness has to be watched as do light feet and fly away ears which can also have dark edges which must be bred out.

The standard requires: LILACS to be pale lilac carried down to the skin. Eyes pink.

46

The Self Red

This is one of the self breeds that is not quite so popular as it once was. It is certainly a most attractive color, being a rich mahogany which must have a fiery look about it. The deeper shades tend to have a poorer undercolor than the lighter shade but as long as the color is even, the undercolor good, and the whole effect has a fiery tone, not a pale color, then that is what to aim for. The eyes should be ruby. Unfortunately type is not very good.

It is an interesting breed because the youngsters can change color, going from light to dark and back again. Some even have a covering of white hairs which disappear leaving a good colored coat. The show life of a young red is extremely limited due to these changes and it does better when it is in adult coat. It is certainly a cavy that is different and one with a challenge that deserves more fanciers taking an interest and trying to improve on what we have rather than trying to breed what we have not.

The standard requires: REDS should be a dark rich color, the same going down to the skin. Feet and ears to match body color. Eyes ruby.

The Self Chocolates

Not readily kept these days which is a pity for this is one of the oldest breeds of selfs having a lovely shade and probably the softest, silkiest coat of all the self breeds. The lovely ruby eyes are most attractive. This is not the largest of the self cavies, tending to be a smaller breed and lacking type although occasionally a good typey one is seen, but very often this is due to the introduction of black blood. The skin of the Chocolate is lighter than the fur and as a result the area of the eyes and nose may appear pinkish due to the finer and shorter hairs. This also applies to the ears which should be smoothed down when young to encourage them to droop. When breeding, care should be taken that litters do not contain babies showing considerable colored hairs as they are inclined to carry cream colored hairs on the shoulders, and around the hips and also patches of red.

The standard requires: CHOCOLATES should be a rich dark color with ears and feet to match body. Eyes ruby.

Any further information can be obtained from either of the addresses listed below. From them you can obtain show rules, guide books and updated standards of perfection of judging and raising cavies.

American Rabbit Breeders Association, Inc.
2401 E. Oakland Avenue
Bloomington, IL 61701

American Cavy Breeders Association
Robert Leishman, Gen. Sec'y Treas.
6560 Upham Street
Arvada, CO 80003

In England, all breeds of cavies have a Specialist Club which caters for their members. They hold Stock Shows throughout the country, ususaly an Adult Stock Show and a Young Stock Show. The Self breeds are catered for by the English Self Cavy Club, usually referred to as the E.S.C.C., and each of the Non-Self Breeds has its own Specialist Club. Any unstandardized or new varieties of rare standardized breeds come under the Rare Varieties Cavy Club, referred to as the R.V.C.C.

The Scottish National Cavy Club caters for the Scottish Fanciers and covers all varieties, and shows are usually held under their rules in Scotland. The South of England has the Southern Cavy Club which again caters for all breeds and has its own rules and regulations under which its shows are held.

The National Cavy Club, referred to as the N.C.C., is recognized as the main Cavy Club and the Parent Society

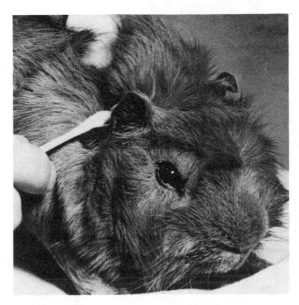

Treat any ear injury as early as possible before it leads to permanent scarring and imperfect ears. The ears are examined closely during judging and it hurts to lose points on a condition which could have been avoided by a little bit of foresight.

to all Specialist Clubs, and is open to all breeds. Shows in general are run under the National Cavy Club Rules unless otherwise stated on the schedule, and as there are one or two differences in the rules of various clubs make sure before you enter your cavies that you are not likely to infringe one of these rules unintentionally. The club relevant to your area will send you a copy of their rules when you join and send your subscription—do read them. Club secretaries are always pleased to help with your queries and a self addressed envelope is always helpful.

There are also many area and local cavy clubs that organize shows at regular intervals. Shows are advertised well in advance in the small livestock magazine called *Fur and Feather* obtainable by order from news agents or by subscription from *Fur and Feather* of Idle, Bradford, Yorkshire. It is published fortnightly and contains information on forthcoming shows and reports on shows held, naming the winners. Stock for sale and wanted together with articles written by breeders are other useful features of the magazine.

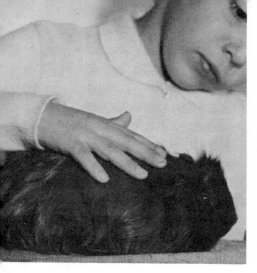

The cost of a guinea pig does not reflect its temperament or quality as a pet. If you are getting a pet for a child your pet shop might be able to offer (see below) such a wide variety of guinea pigs that it might be difficult to make up your mind as to what kind you want.

Buying The Guinea Pig

It is best to purchase an animal when it is six to eight weeks old, weighing 8 to 12 ounces. By this time it is fully independent of its mother, readily adaptable to the new surroundings and eager to make new friends. From this time to breeding season, it is a playful pet and kittenish in manners. Its life span is about eight years when given proper care and feeding.

It makes little difference whether you get a male or female. Assuming you are getting just one for a pet, you will be satisfied with either sex. Two females are compatible and get along, but two males may cause you trouble for

(1) The proper way to hold your pet cavy requires the use of both hands. Since cavies are almost never vicious, you don't have to worry about controlling the head. Hold the animal firmly around the bottom and don't panic if it begins using its feet. (2) Cavies can be left outside if they have sufficient water. If you use a wire cage with an open wire bottom, it can be placed over grass and the guinea pigs can have fresh grass for a meal.

1 2

a while. Should you buy a pair, by all means get a breeding hutch with them as you will need one. A trio consisting of one male and two females is better if you wish to raise young with the possibility of selling them to the petshop in your neighborhood.

A litter usually consists of three to six young, the average being three. Gestation period is sixty to seventy days. Well-developed females may become sexually mature at the very young age of a month or six weeks, but should not be bred until they are at least five months of age.

When looking for a good cavy, make sure the animal has large and brilliant eyes, sound teeth and a good coat. As each type has individual coats, if you want an English, look for the sleek, statiny coat; an Abyssinian should have a rough textured coat with noticeable rosettes, the more the better; while the Peruvian should have long, silky hair. Select an animal that has broad shoulders, eats at a forward angle, and is active and full of spirit.

Bathing

This must not be done frequently, only if your cavy has been ill and has recovered and is smelly and dirty, or if you want to show it. A plastic bowl is probably the easiest thing to use. Half-fill the bath with warm water and genly lower the cavy's hindlegs into the water. Allow it to sit. You should continue to support it, with your hand under it. With your other hand, sponge the coat and lather the shampoo avoiding the face and eyes. Rinse off with warm water and wrap the cavy in a dry towel and gently rub it. Use a hairdryer to dry it completely. A soft bristle brush, not a stiff nylon one, should be used. Do not put the cavy back into the hutch until you have cleaned the cage out thoroughly and the cavy has cooled down and dried off from the bath, otherwise it may catch pneumonia.

(Left) A nicely designed home for cavies with automatic feeders and waterers. Remember (below) that your cavy has a small stomach and should never be offered more food than it can eat or the food will deteriorate and might cause offensive odors.

Housing

Like any pet animal, the guinea pig should have a home of its own. Should you give it the run of your home, care must be taken to look around before closing a door or he may have followed you and been trapped. Being affectionate, they seek out your companionship and try to stay close by.

A guinea pig cage is not expensive for the standard models which are equipped with feed and water dish, some type of shelf on which the pet can climb and rest, and a bottom sliding compartment for easy cleaning.

Many suitable containers can be made and of various material. A wooden box may be cut down to a size of 20″ × 18″ × 12″. Some type of removable tray should be arranged which can be removed for easy cleaning and should be covered with sawdust, wood shavings, straw, hay or any of the commercial cat litters. A small rake or slotted kitchen spoon is most handy to remove the droppings.

A heavy mesh can be utilized nicely to make a cage. Make a framework of four uprights attached to the top and bottom frame to make the outline of a box, then cover the sides and one end with the mesh. A pan of some kind large enough to cover the bottom, but small enough to easily remove, can be placed into the cage. The conventional cat pan is very good to use. In the mesh cage, two sides should be covered to prevent draft. A low platform can be attached to one side for the animal to rest upon. If the cage is large enough, insert a small wooden or cardboard box on its side with one end open and your pet will go into the secluded place to seek a dark area to sleep.

With a cage of this kind, you can take the animal outdoors during warm and sunny days, invert the cage over him and allow him the run of a small area on either ground or lawn. He will munch on the bits of grass and thoroughly enjoy himself. Although by nature he is a burrowing animal, domesticity seems to have removed this habit so he will not try to escape by means of tunneling. If the sun is too warm, move the cage to a shadier spot or cover it in some way with newspapers or a heavy towel.

He should have a water dish filled with clean water at all times. If the dish is affixed by means of a wire brace, it can be lifted out and cleaned easily. Metal dishes for water should not be used. An ideal dish is a heavy one of china or pottery, shallow enough to allow the pet to drink but firm enough that he won't be able to turn it over.

The feeding dish should also be of china or pottery and washed out in hot water at least every third day.

As a general guide, one cavy needs two square feet of floor space. Some people keep their cavy in an old disused aquarium, which is a good idea as the guinea pig can be observed at all times, the housing can be washed and dried out well, it will be protected from drafts and the floor area is sufficient for one cavy depending on the size of the aquarium. More cavies can live together in a bigger aquarium. Use your own discretion and remember that no animal (including you) takes kindly to overcrowding.

The important thing is to bear in mind when you are looking for housing is that the cavy must have a draft free, dry place to live with a good circulation of air. If your area is damp and there is a lot of condensation, then heating must be provided. Heaters should be the long tubular kind that is fully enclosed and that will not cause a fire. Fuel oil and kerosene heaters are dangerous, apart from the possibility of the fumes affecting your pet. Open electric heaters, like the fuel oil heaters are a hazard. Electric lighting is another essential, especially during the dark, winter months. Be careful where you place your cage or hutch. For example, a garage that houses a car, is not a place to be considered, as the fumes from a car exhaust could prove lethal and asphyxiate your cavy.

Handling

When you pick up your cavy, you must take care not to pick it up by the shoulders or the top part of its body. Its weight should be supported or the cavy could twist and injure itself internally. Also you must not drop your cavy because it will land on its head first and it will die. Slide your hand under its body, palm up, and lift the cavy slowly, with its chest and forelegs resting on your wrist and your other hand supporting and steadying it. The more you handle your pet, the more it will become accustomed to you. The babies should be handled as soon as possible and they will respond by becoming tame and demonstrative.

The care, feeding and maintenance of a cavy are the same whether the animal is of show quality or pet quality. Buy the best cavy you can. You'll be glad you did.

Feeding

Feeding is a simple matter as guinea pigs are vegetarians and eat fruits and vegetables, rabbit pellets, bread and even small pieces of dog biscuits.

If you have just the one animal, you must remember that it is a tiny animal with a small stomach. You will not, therefore, put in whole apples, whole carrots, or several big pieces of lettuce. Instead, use the fruit or vegetable you are serving at your own meal, and cut off tiny slices or bits like a slice of apple, a portion of a leaf of cabbage or lettuce or a slice of carrot. Anything he does not eat (outside of dry pellets) should be removed daily and replaced with fresh food. You can vary the daily food with a bit of apple and lettuce one day, a potato paring and carrot top next day. Yes, he will like the tops of most green vegetables.

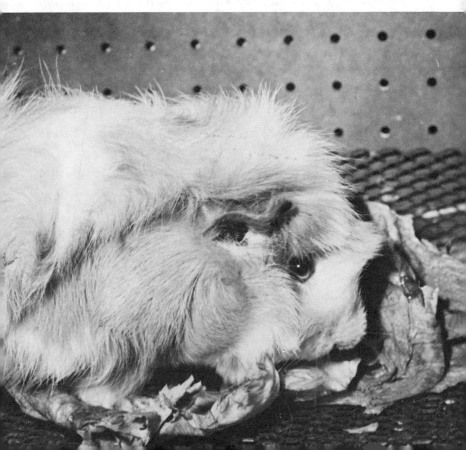

Vegetables most acceptable include carrots, carrot top, raw string bean, potato slice or paring, a portion of raw tomato—the list is long. All green leafy vegetables are good, with the outside leaves the best, but make sure the stalks and leaves are clean and washed, then dried. Never use food taken directly from the refrigerator.

Further addition to the diet can include dandelion, kale, grass clippings and beets. Try different vegetables and you will find he rejects very few.

Care must be taken with green vegetables as an overabundance given constantly may produce diarrhea. Should this occur, cut the vegetables down considerably, you may even eliminate them for a day, then half portions for a while until the condition is eliminated. Too much greens make very loose and even liquid waste, which in turn may produce an odor in the shavings or litter used.

I have found that a very small portion of one green vegetable and a bit of fruit every other day keeps my cavies in good condition, especially if they have a constant supply of dry foods. In fact, a game can be made of feeding the vegetable—pick up the animal and allow him to run to the curve of your arm where he will cuddle down like a "teddy bear" in a crouch position with front paws held up. Offer him a bit of food and he will clamp his little paws around it and munch happily away.

Dry foods consist of:

Grains—which include oatmeal, barley, bran, whole wheat, corn meal, or any grain you may have available. Oatmeal is best as most homes keep this on hand. A scant teaspoonful is ample, given occasionally. Other grains should be used proportionately.

I have found that the good grades of **rabbit pellets** will contain not only the acceptable grains, but alfalfa, soybean oil meals, and even vitamin compounds which make them an ideal food. A dish may be provided for the pellets but do not fill it to capacity for the animal may shove much of it out in his attempt to get the pellets. It is better to give small amounts, then refill the dish as necessary, to prevent litter from getting accumulated in the food dish. The dish should be wiped out and given a hot water wash at least weekly. An exception is, of course, should you wish to be away for several days, then sufficient food should be left. Pellets and other dry foods should be stored in a clean sealed container.

Other acceptable foods include bits of bread, cracker, peanuts (shelled, of course). Try out various items of food and if taken, add to the diet. Have the fun of having any pet is feeding new items of food and having them accepted. *A caution on this*—until the animal is accustomed to the new food, give sparingly, and eliminate one of the other foods. Your pet can eat just so much and the balance will either spoil, decay, or wilt which means it must be thrown away.

Occasionally, especially during winter months, I put a drop of cod-liver oil on the dry food where it is absorbed and then consumed.

Many people make a task out of feeding their pet or pets—*don't!* You know what types of food are acceptable so use a little common sense and if you don't have one particular vegetable, substitute another. Judge the amount of food necessary. If there is too much left over, then you are feeding too much. If the dish is empty and the vegetable consumed entirely with the animal seeking more food, then you are not feeding enough. Some cavies eat more than others, much like people. You and you alone can determine the right amount and volumes of instructions won't help you unless you watch the pet for a few weeks and determine his needs.

When you feed your cavy, remember the following factors and use them as a guide.

It must have vitamin C every day.

It must have hay every day.

It must have a good grain staple every day.

It must have water every day.

Never feed it frozen food taken from the refrigerator or food that is stale and moldy, or your cavy will develop intestinal disorders and when other complications occur (for example pneumonia or diarrhea), you will lose your pet and companion that you could have had for seven years. The following is a discussion of these important food requirements in greater detail.

Vitamin C is very important as the cavy cannot live without it. It *must* have vitamin C. Guinea pigs, like people and apes, but unlike dogs and other mammals, cannot manufacture their own Vitamin C requirements. It can be found in greens, fruit and roots. Carrots, for example, are very rich in vitamins, sugar and oil. They also contain calcium and iron. Beets are good bodybuilders (not the beet tops though, as they contain oxalic acid). Spinach adds variety to the diet and can be used as a treat. Celery should be thoroughly washed and only used occasionally with pieces of apple. When you are training your pet, you could feed it these treats as rewards. All the above vegetables contain vitamin C.

Centuries ago sailors used to get scurvy from a deficiency of this vitamin in their diet, because they could not get a supply of fresh fruit and vegetables on their voyages. Your guinea pig is like old-time sailors in this regard—it too will get scurvy if you deprive it of this essential vitamin.

The next important requirement is hay without which your pet cannot digest what it has eaten. Without it, it will chew its own hair and will not develop or grow. Provide only the best feeding hay. There should be no mold or dust. Smell the hay and you will be able to tell immediately if it should be given "the thumbs up." Besides providing an excellent source of warmth in the winter months, if it is used for bedding, it is a valuable source of protein, carbohydrates and minerals.

Note that the hay must be dried out for six months before

it is used, otherwise it will be damp and detrimental to the well being and health of your cavy.

Grains, including oats, barley, wheat, bran and pellets, are necessary sources of bodybuilding and energy giving food. These are recommended for young, growing cavies, but they are fattening and if you feed your grown pet too much of them without balancing its diet with other foods, it will become obese.

Water is absolutely essential particularly in the summer or if your sow is pregnant. Water bottles made especially for this purpose can be obtained from most pet shops. Water supplied in pots is unsuitable, because the boar will probably kick over the container if there is a sow present in a display of masculine virility and strength. Any guinea pig could easily knock the container over, and the housing would become damp and wet.

Your cavy will be a healthy animal if you take care not to feed it or leave any rotting, moldy food in its living space. Guinea pig pellets should be hard and firm and any green vegetable going yellow or soft is unsuitable.

Ideally, your pet should be fed in the morning and evening, although the occasional daytime tidbit will probably be appreciated. The main meal should be at night, when most cavies eat most of their food. The main rule about feeding your pet is: when in doubt, don't, for although your cavy should selectively known what to eat, it is better not to take chances.

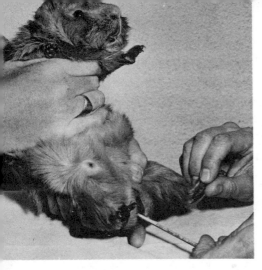

If your cavy is ill, take it to a veterinarian. He may take its temperature (left) to see whether it has an infection. (Below) If your pet cavy is not acting normally you should isolate it from your other pets until it is well.

Ailments

There are several common ailments, some of them being preventable by proper care. A cavy that is listless, huddled in a corner, refusing food, with dull matted coat is a sick animal. Check the condition of the cage. Is it in the draft, has the water dish been overturned and the animal become chilled, is the cage in too cold a place? The guinea pig can usually take changes of temperature, but dampness and drafts can be too much. Should the ailment continue after your home treatment, go to your local veterinarian but don't wait too long, as the sicker the animal, the harder to treat.

(1) Black Dutch cavy. (2) Self Lilac cavy.

3
4

(3) Self Golden, dark-eyed cavy. (4) Self Cream cavy.

Should the animal hover in a corner with heaving sides, with over-brilliant eyes, possibly watering, and running nose, he probably has taken a cold. Throw a woolen cloth over the side and top of the cage and keep the bottom litter dry and clean. Don't feed too much and eliminate the green vegetable to a third of the normal portion. Warm a teaspoonful of fresh milk and pour it over a small piece of bread, allowing the bread to soak up the milk and become moist before you offer it. He may or may not eat immediately, but after a few hours try again.

Diarrhea is caused by too many green vegetables fed too often. In addition to the watery and smelly stool, the stomach may become bloated, the pet refuses to eat and the hair assumes a shaggy appearance. Eliminate the greens entirely for a few days and use only dry grains and pellets until the stool returns to normal. During the course of the ailment, keep an eye on the bottom of the cage and remove as much debris as possible, replacing with clean litter. When the vegetables are returned to the diet, cut the amount to one-third and very gradually return to normal.

Improper feeding may result in scurvy which is caused by insufficient vitamins. The addition of cabbage (green outer leaves) and tomatoes help in cleaning up this condition, but a vitamin supplement is best.

Guinea pigs, like dogs and cats, often have fleas, which cause them to scratch. Any good flea powder may be applied, following instructions on the label of the can. Throw out shavings and give the cage a hot water wash. If you are using a wooden box, get the flea powder into the cracks and corners, allow it to remain a short while, then, using a whisk broom, remove all powder possible.

Your cavy, when it is properly cared for, will be a very healthy animal, but occasionally it is necessary to know what to use in treating your ailing pet. If you are confused or in any doubt, do not hesitate to take your guinea pig to a veterinarian. Most pet shops stock a medi-kit for intestinal disorders, which is inexpensive, but most of the remedies are "human remedies" used in a diluted form for the treatment of your cavy.

The following is a discussion of various pests and ailments for your information.

Lice are pests, not an ailment. Fortunately, guinea pig lice do not attack human beings. These small parasites live on skin debris. As the cavy is very susceptible to chemicals, you must be careful of any preparation that is used as an insecticide. Louse powders used for dogs and cats can sometimes be too overpowering. Pesticidal agents formulated specifically for use in eliminating lice and certain other parasites are available at well-stocked pet shops.

Mites are small parasites that burrow into the skin of the animal, causing much distress. The animal becomes continuously agitated. Your pet will become miserable and cry out in pain. A pregnant sow will most certainly abort her litter if she is afflicted. Treatment must be given immediately. Paratox or Cuprex or A-200 are all liquids that are available from a pharmacy. However, the cavy must be dipped in a solution of ONE PART medication to SEVENTY TWO PARTS warm water. Ignore the label directions on the bottle, as this is for human usage. Do not rinse the solution off but gently dry your cavy with a towel and dry off with the hairdryer. Most pet shops will supply a pesticidal soap, but this must be rinsed off thoroughly after bathing your cavy with it.

Eye Injuries and Infections

As the cavy's bedding consists of wood shavings or dried grass there is a possibility that it may injure its eyes while burrowing. Some seed could also be lodged under the eyelid, which could cause it to become inflamed, or the eye itself could become cloudy. Treat it with a mild eye ointment twice a day until the cloudiness has disappeared. A very minute amount is necessary. Allergies can be caused

(1) Young Beige cavy. (2) Himalayan cavies.

3

(3) American Crested Golden cavy. (4) White Crested Cavy.

4

by pollen or dust. If the eyes run or water continually, half a teaspoon of salt to half a pint of cooled boiled water stored in a clean bottle and applied by means of an eyedropper three times a day should clear up the symptoms of this allergy.

Torn Ears or Cuts

Something may frighten your cavy or a mother may run over her babies if she is startled. A solution of salt and water, as recommended in the allergy section, can be used for cleaning the cuts. Some antiseptic powder can then be dusted over the exposed area.

Abscesses can be caused by hard knocks or fighting. An abscess usually begins around the cheek. Leave it alone. It will grow larger, become softer and eventually burst. Wipe the fluid away and bathe the area in the recommended salt-water solution. Repeat this each day until all of the matter has been removed and the wound heals. It must be kept clean. Abscesses are not fatal and treatment by antibiotics is not recommended.

Compaction of the Rectum

This is when the droppings compact in the rectum. Vaseline should be applied around the lump. A tissue or a dry cloth could be used to remove it piece by piece.

Diarrhea and Intestinal Upsets

The animal should not be fed any greens, fruits or vegetables until its stool has returned to normal. Hay and bran dampened slightly with water should be given to the sick cavy for food. Provide water with vitamin C added to it. Enteritis, caused by rotten food, can be confused with diarrhea. This is fatal and should be treated by a veterinarian if it is not too late.

Your pet shop will have special products for maintaining your guinea pig in good health. (1) Guinea pig vitamins can be mixed in with the food. (2) Tasty guinea pig treat is useful in training. (3) Natural cedar shavings deodorize and maintain a healthy cage bottom. (4) Guinea pig food mixtures guarantee the balanced diet your guinea pig requires. (5) Sprays for hamsters can be used for guinea pigs too; they kill fleas, ticks and mites and deodorize.

1

2

3

5

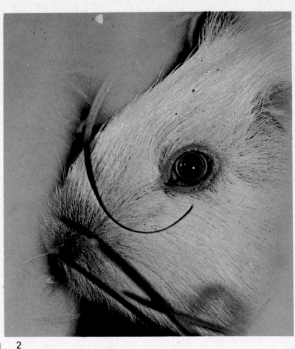

1 2

(1) Head-on view of a Tortie and White. (2) Lilac self with red eyes. (3) Crested cavies. (4) Sheltie, or Silkie. (5) Tri-colored Peruvian long-hair being groomed. These show-quality cavies require constant brushing with a soft brush. (6) These are just six of the different color varieties in which guinea pigs have been developed. There are strict color standards for cavies should you care to enter a contest.

3

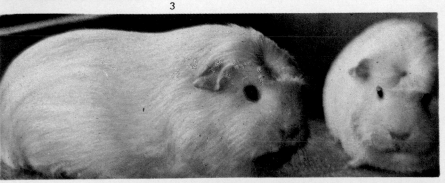

4

5

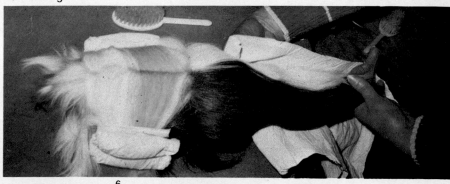

6

Food can be offered as a reward in the training (left) of your pet cavy. The person training the cavy should be the one who regularly feeds the animal (below). In this way, the cavy will recognize the person as a friend and will react better than it would to a stranger.

Training

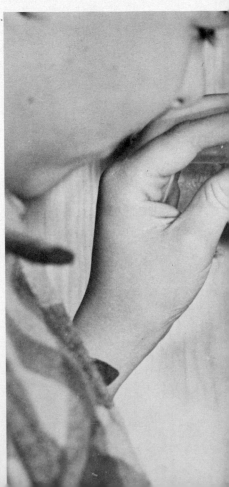

To properly lift a guinea pig, use both hands, one beneath the animal and the other encircling his body near the neck and shoulders. After he becomes used to your hands, sit him in you lap or in the bend of your arm and allow him to run up your arm to your shoulder.

He can easily be taught to raise up on his hind legs and eat from your fingers. Hold the food just high enough that he has to reach up for it. By using special tidbits of his choice, he will soon know that to get the bit, he must sit up, so as soon as he does sit up, give him the food. After he accomplished this, hold him on the palm of your left hand

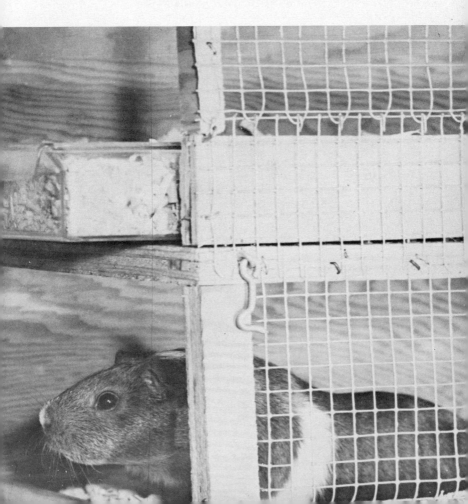

1

(1) Tri-colored Peruvian Long-haired cavy. (2) Self Lilac cavy. (3) Self Cream cavy. (4) If you want to breed rare colors and coat characteristics you must know the exact parentage of your offspring. This means that they cannot be kept in colonies but must be isolated. (5) Silver Agouti cavy. (6) Tortie and White cavy. (7) Self Beige. The quality of a cavy depends upon its adherence to a standard. Its price depends upon its quality as a show animal.

2

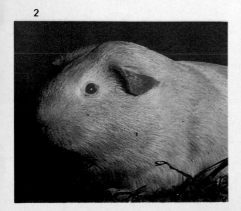

3

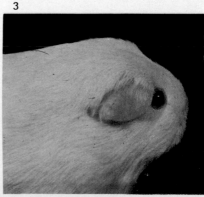

4

5 6

7

and get him to sit up. Be careful that you don't drop him so use your forefinger to prop him in back and your thumb in front. Gradually, as he better balances himself, lower the forefinger and thumb until he will sit up without help.

He will also 'waltz' for you. Using your forefinger on your right hand, use an easy shove motion at the left shoulder of your pet to get him to move in that direction. With your right hand holding a favorite bit of food, bring your fingers just far enough to his right side that he has to turn in the direction you are shoving. As he turns, keep your fingers with the food just out of his reach until he has gone in a circle. Then give him the food. When he starts the circle at the touch of your hand at his shoulder, make him go two circles before releasing the food. When he has caught on to this trick, you can really show him off to your friends.

1

(1) Training your cavy begins with hand-feeding. Keep the pet cavy hungry so that it will immediately respond to food when offered from your hand. (2) An ideal setup for beginners who want to breed cavies. (3) The difference between males and females becomes very obvious when you press on the abdomen. (4) A sow can be kept with her young as long as they suckle (as shown here), but they must be removed after weaning, as they become sexually mature and may mate with her.

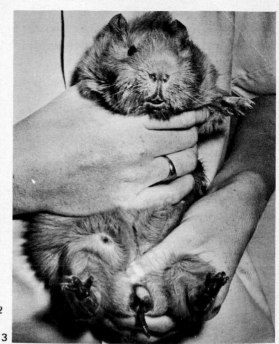

2

3

4

Cavies are such sweet, hardy, even-tempered pets that it's difficult to think of them as potential money-makers. But breeding them for pet shops to re-sell, or as laboratory animals, can be a rewarding venture if you need supplementary income. They can even be fed grass to supplement their regular diet.

(Left) These cavies snuggled up in a bowl and had their litter in this same bowl! A better way to breed and maintain your pet cavies is shown below. The partitions are removable.

Breeding

These animals enjoy a family life and a male with several females seems very content. In fact, so content that when the females bear their young, they can still be kept together. The father does not harm the young.

Four or five sows can run with one boar, but never put two boars together where there are sows present or even within smelling distance. Even if you used the containers that you had taken from a sow-inhabited cage they would fight. Cavies do not breed as quickly as rabbits and may take many months before they decide to mate. In the breed-

(1) Unlike these baby mice and almost any other rodent, guinea pigs are not born blind and helpless. New-born mice do not open their eyes for almost two weeks. (2) This sow and her litter of four identical offspring are all Silver Agouti. The outcome of a mating between two pure-bred guinea pigs can be predicted with confidence. (3) Indiscriminate breeding results in an unpredictable outcome. This cavy sow had all mixed piglets. Guinea pigs have a gestation period of about 65 days and have one to six young at a time. The young are born furred.

2
3

87

ing process, there are three schools of thought. These are:
Method one: Some breeders prefer to leave the pregnant sows with the boar. However, the babies could be trampled on when the boar tries to mate with the other sows or with the sow that has just delivered. The latter is called postpartum mating and it is bad because the sow should have a rest between litters and not be treated as a breeding machine.

Method two: Some breeders prefer to remove the pregnant sow to another hutch before she is due to give birth. Many breeders feel that this is the best method. The only disadvantage to this is that she might abort if she is unhappy in her new and unfamiliar surrounding. It would be better to put the boar with her for awhile or at least until she is due and then remove him. This makes the transition between the breeding and the littering pen an easier one.

Method three: Some breeders prefer to keep one pregnant sow with one boar which is fine if there is enough room for them both to exercise. Some breeders routinely keep the boar away from the babies, just in case he might harm them.

Gestation period is around sixty-five days, litters consisting of from three to six young. The female can bear young four times a year up until she is six years old, although she is considered to have reached her prime at three; a male a year or so longer.

Babies are born with their eyes open, with the little bodies covered in soft fur. They romp and play when a few days old while the parents look on. The youngsters are weaned when they are five or six weeks old. They are able to eat solid food a few days after birth. Born with upstanding ears, gradually they assume a drooped appearance.

Feeding and Fostering the Babies

If the sow dies then the litter can be hand reared. Milk powder mixed with warm milk and fed with an eyedropper

An adequate setup of breeding cages for cavies. Note the special compartment which provides an area protected from draft for the newly born babies.

can be used to feed the babies every two hours. Ideally this should be through the night, but one feeding will suffice. Do not squeeze the food into their mouths, as they will then choke. They will learn to suck at the dropper. Also mix some bran or brown bread with milk and place this in a shallow container. This mixture must be renewed frequently and the dish kept clean. You will have to clean the faces of the babies, and the mother would normally do this. After a few days you can start feeding the babies greens and roots, but you should mince up the carrots and the beets for awhile. Babies are usually fed by the mother for four weeks and they should then be separated by sex, otherwise the boars could become very aggressive in the company of the sows of the litter. Boars can be put together providing there are no sows present. See to it that as you expand your guinea pig collection, you expand the living space.

1

(1) While 65 days is an average gestation period of cavies, some color varieties take 68-75 days. The maximum recorded litter size is 12, but there have been cases in which only one baby was born. Unfortunately the mother has only one pair of nipples. The youngsters normally wean after three weeks. (2) A White-collared cavy is the result of a breeding that was unplanned. However, this strain was fixed and it is now possible to predict which mating will produce more White-collars. (3) This Sheltie has a wrapper at its backside to keep its coat clean and to protect it from being torn. This is a technique of show people.

2 3

A white mother cavy (rosette type) with her litter of three days in age. She is suckling a brown colored baby cavy. A mother cavy (below) protects her young although her baby cavy is already capable of feeding on other foods besides milk.

It's Up to You Now

Like any pet, this one can be a lot of fun or a lot of work—if you accept the little fellow as a pet and new member of the family, he will respond to your kindness with his endearing habits. He needs certain amounts of food and water, housing quarters and a place to call his own when he will prefer his own company. During that time, leave him alone. During eating, allow him to feed without petting him or picking him up. Handle him gently and teach the children to do likewise. Now you can thoroughly enjoy your new guinea pig.

It really doesn't matter whether you want to raise show-quality cavies or just long-haired Peruvian cavies which will end up as common housepets. Cavies are fun . . . and profitable. This Peruvian guinea pig is one of the early (1940's) prototypes of the Peruvian long-haired show beauties.